D1264945

Cover illustration: Fairey Gordon K1743, fitted with a Panther engine, makes a low pass for the photographer. The not inconsiderable size of this machine is easily appreciated. Note the lower wingtip lights, with flare brackets beneath. In common with most other Fairey designs, the Gordon was available in both sea- and landplane versions. (Ian D. Huntley)

1. N225 (F890) was the second Fairey IIIF prototype, and this fine study reveals its elegant lines. A great deal of experimental work was undertaken by IIIFs, and at least two were on permanent development work: S1532, for example, tested flotation gear, bomb carriers, airscrews, and even a three-float system. It ended its days as a catapult dummy. (Ian D. Huntley)

VINTAGE WARBIRDS No 3

R.A.F.
between the Wars

RAYMOND LAURENCE RIMELL

ARMS AND ARMOUR PRESS

Introduction

Published in 1985 by Arms and Armour Press
2-6 Hampstead High Street, London NW3 1QQ.

Distributed in the United States by
Sterling Publishing Co. Inc., 2 Park Avenue,
New York, N.Y. 10016.

British Library Cataloguing in Publication Data:
Rimell, Raymond Laurence
R.A.F. Between the Wars – (Vintage warbirds; no. 3)
1. Great Britain. *Royal Air Force* – History
2. Airplanes, Military – Great Britain – History
I. Title   II. Series
623.74'6'0941   TL685.3
ISBN 0-85368-703-X

Editing, design and artwork by Roger Chesneau.
Typesetting by Typesetters (Birmingham) Ltd.
Printed and bound in Italy.

After the signing of the Armistice in 1918, which ended one of the bloodiest wars in history, the fledgling Royal Air Force was looking forward to a number of promising new aircraft designs then being developed by several of Britain's leading manufacturers. However, postwar demobilization and severe cuts in financial backing from the Government decimated RAF strength so much that the new air arm was forced to compromise with regard to its equipment. Thus it was that those few squadrons which remained operational by 1920 were generally to be found equipped with ex-wartime types such as the Bristol Fighter (the subject of Vintage Warbirds No. 4), DH9A, Sopwith Snipe and Vickers Vimy.

Through the first decade of peace, the RAF contracted out various tenders to British manufacturers for general-purpose machines – multi-role aircraft which could be easily adapted for differing operational requirements. Such strictures resulted, it has since been argued, in aircraft development being retarded by the production of machines scarcely more technically advanced than those of the war years: for example, whilst such classic fighters as the Bulldog, Siskin, Gamecock and Fury were manoeuvrable, easy to fly and aesthetically pleasing, they were obsolete well before their withdrawal. History shows that, had the Second World War broken out a few years earlier, the RAF would have entered the conflict with many of its aircraft not vastly superior to those used during the First.

Although the period covered in this volume is commonly referred to as 'between the wars', the decades between the global conflicts were hardly peaceful for the RAF, which was almost continually involved in some war, somewhere in the world. 'Golden era' is another oft-used term, chosen, one suspects, because it saw the biplane reach its peak and the emergence of Gloster and Supermarine high-speed racing seaplanes and of prototypes of warplanes which would go on to achieve immortality in 'Hitler's war'.

For this volume, the author has striven to include illustrations which have not previously been published and photographs which depict less well-known types. With the help of colleague Ian Huntley, some emphasis has been placed on valuable Fairey archival material; this has yielded splendid portraits of aircraft both familiar and largely forgotten. As a result, there are several views of naval aircraft – but of course it may be noted that the Fleet Air Arm was part of the RAF up to 1937.

As usual, the author is indebted to fellow enthusiasts for the provision of photographs, and thanks are therefore accorded to Ian D. Huntley, Bruce Robertson and, from the RAF Museum, Gp. Capt. W. S. O. Randle, Reg Mack, Dave Roberts and Tim Calloway; thanks are due too, to Mrs S. Walsh. Finally, the author would like to dedicate this book to the memory of the late Mike Twite.

Raymond Laurence Rimell

◀2
2. The best known 'interwar' RAF types could be found among the large Hawker Hart family of two-seaters; these are Hawker Audaxes of No. 13 Squadron. Designed for army co-operation duties, the Audax carried long rods which picked up messages from the ground, earning it the sobriquet 'the 'Art with the 'ook'! (Bruce Robertson)

▲3

3. Sopwith Snipes in postwar service, sporting the familiar aluminium dope/natural metal finish of the period. Production of this aircraft continued until early 1919, and the Snipe remained in service as the RAF's standard single-seat fighter until 1926. It was withdrawn from service the following year. (RAF Museum)

4. JR6925 was an ex-Nieuport Nighthawk converted by the Gloucestershire Aircraft Co. into the Mars VI which boasted a more powerful engine. Only a few examples of the Nighthawk were purchased by the Air Ministry and, in 1923, these were allocated to Nos. 1 and 8 Squadrons in Mesopotamia for trials under tropical conditions. (RAF Museum)

▼4

5▲

5. The Armstrong Whitworth Siskin was the standard RAF fighter of the late 1920s, and twelve squadrons operated the type. It was generally liked by pilots, and few aircraft could equal its aerobatic agility, among the top exponents of which was No. 43 Squadron, whose 'tied-together' Siskin formations thrilled crowds at prewar flying displays.

6. 'The Bulldog breed'. This purposeful-looking fighter was another popular mount for pilots with a penchant for aerobatics. The Bristol Bulldog entered service in 1929 and within two years equipped no fewer than nine squadrons, remaining the most widely used RAF fighter type for half a decade. (RAF Museum)

6▼

▲7

7. Some measure of the Bulldog's excellence is attested to by the fact that export versions were operated by the air forces of Denmark, Estonia, Finland, Latvia, Sweden and Australia. A two-seat version, for training, was built in some numbers for the RAF. The Bulldog was withdrawn from service in 1937. (Bruce Robertson)

8. The Fairey Fantôme was built at the company factory at Hayes for the Belgian Government's International Fighter Competition. The aircraft shown, F6, was placed on the civil register as G-ADIF and demonstrated at the Hendon SBAC show on 1 July 1935. Sixteen days later, at Evère, Brussels, the aircraft crashed, killing its pilot S. H. G. Trower. This rare view shows the clean installation of the 925hp Hispano-Suiza engine. (Ian D. Huntley)

▼8

9. The graceful, flowing lines of the Fairey Fantôme can be appreciated to the full in this study of L7045, which was evaluated for RAF service from February 1938 through to June of the following year. In the event, Fantômes did not see production. (Ian D. Huntley)

10. One of the stars at the 1923 SBAC show was the new fleet fighter, the Fairey Flycatcher, being studied here by Winston Churchill. The aircraft served aboard all the Royal Navy aircraft carriers of the day and was the last fighter to be flown off gun turret platforms of capital ships. Its small dimensions made it ideal for carrier use, and although it did not feature folding wings the airframe was easily dismantled for storage. (Ian D. Huntley)

11. To the chagrin of enthusiasts and modellers, documentation for unit markings applied to fleet fighters of the 1920s is virtually non-existent. These Flycatchers are thought to be from HMS *Eagle*'s 401 Flight; the fuselage bands and wheel discs appear to be black and white, as is the fin of N9923. Note the different style of serial applied to the rearmost machine. (RAF Museum)

12. A Fairey Flycatcher and Blackburn Darts aboard an unidentified British aircraft carrier during the mid-1920s. The Dart, although unlovely to look at, had good deck-landing qualities and the first touch-down on a carrier at night was made by a Dart on 1 July 1926 by Flt. Lt. Boyce. (Ian D. Huntley)

13. A splendid 1923 portrait of a Fairey Flycatcher Mk. 1. The zero dihedral of the lower mainplanes was a distinctive feature of this twin-gun fleet fighter. Powered by a 400hp Armstrong Siddeley Jaguar, the Flycatcher was extremely manoeuvrable and, according to pilots, extremely noisy, rivalling the note of the Harvard when diving! (Ian D. Huntley)

▲11   ▼12

▲14　▼15

14. A line-up of Gloster Gamecocks of No. 23 Squadron. The Gamecock was a development of the Grebe in which the Bristol Jupiter radial engine replaced the Armstrong Siddeley Jaguar. Like its predecessor, the Gamecock suffered from wing flutter which was only overcome by fitting extra outboard interplane struts to support the upper wing extensions. (RAF Museum)

15. A closer view of No. 23 Squadron Gamecocks showing their red and blue squadron markings. The Gamecock formed the equipment of five RAF units in the 1920s and was an excellent aerobatic mount. In 1931 the aircraft was withdrawn from service. Note that the aircraft in the background of this photograph lacks the large spinner as fitted to J8092. (RAF Museum)

16. J7357 was a Gloster Grebe Mk. II and is seen here undergoing taxying trials – at least, one presumes that pilots of the day did not fly wearing their service caps! Derived from the Nieuport Nighthawk of 1918, the Grebe inherited much of that aircraft's excellent handling qualities and it equipped five RAF squadrons until its front-line withdrawal in 1928.

17. An unidentified Grebe, c1924. The type carved its niche in aeronautical history at the 1925 Hendon Pageant when a formation team from No. 25 Squadron at Hawkinge used ground-to-air and air-to-air radio transmission for the first time. Part of an R/T conversation between the flight leader, Sqn. Ldr. A. Peck, and HM King George V was broadcast by the BBC.

18. One to baffle the aeroplane spotters! N227 was the number applied to the Gloster SS35 Gnatsnapper, which was designated Mks. I, II and III in succession with Mercury, Jaguar and Kestrel radials. This neat little aircraft never entered production and remains very much a 'rare bird'. (RAF Museum)

16▲

17▲   18▼

▲19

▲20 ▼21

19. The first production Gloster Gauntlets were delivered to No. 19 Squadron during May 1935, and this popular aircraft went on to equip no fewer than eighteen units. A number went to Palestine with No. 6 Squadron and were used in operations against Arab tribes. More popular with service pilots than its well-known successor the Gladiator, the Gauntlet was a superb aerobatic machine. (RAF Museum)

20. The Gloster Gladiator will forever remain one of the legends of the RAF. It was the last biplane fighter to see RAF service and marked the transition from biplane to advanced high-speed monoplane designs. The Gladiator employed several new features for its time, including flaps, a multi-gun armament and an enclosed cockpit. Thirty-one squadrons were equipped with the type, and Gladiators saw successful operational use in the early years of the Second World War. (RAF Museum)

21. A trolley-accumulator gets the Gladiator's 840hp Bristol Mercury engine going in this dramatic study. The Gladiator first entered RAF service with No. 3 Squadron, based at Tangmere, in February 1937. With its greater wing loading and advanced features, the Gladiator's handling characteristics suffered slightly in comparison with earlier types, yet it was pleasant to fly. (Bruce Robertson)

22. Perhaps the best known, and arguably the finest, RAF fighter of the 'tween years' period was the Hawker Fury. K3731 was on the strength of No. 43 Squadron ('The Fighting Cocks') and bears the black and white checks of that unit. The fin and tailplane are in the flight colours, possibly blue in this case. Note the highly polished metal panels and cowlings. (RAF Museum)

23. A neat formation of Hawker Fury IIs of No. 25 Squadron, *c*1937, with the CO's aircraft nearest the camera; the squadron colour is black. This unit was the first to receive the Fury Mk. II, in December 1936, and was followed by Nos. 41 and 42. The famous No. 1 Squadron did not operate this type, but the newly formed units flew Fury IIs from March 1937. (RAF Museum)

24. Fury IIs of No. 25 Squadron; note the wheel spats, which serve to distinguish the type. Powered by the 640hp Rolls-Royce Kestrel VI, the Fury II was one of the finest aircraft of its time and variants were delivered to the air forces of South Africa, Norway, Persia, Portugal, Spain and Yugoslavia. (RAF Museum)

22▲

23▲   24▼

25. A mixed formation of Hawker Ospreys and Hawker Nimrods, naval versions of, respectively, the Hart two-seater and Fury. These aircraft are from No. 800 Squadron, c1935. Although the Nimrod is generally regarded as a navalized Fury, the machines actually differed a good deal and had distinctly separate origins.

26. The Avro 504N, developed from the famous wartime 504K, was known as the 'Lynx Avro' on account of its uprated powerplant. Other differences included ailerons of reduced area and an improved and simplified undercarriage. F8713 belonged to an unidentified training unit, c1930. (RAF Museum)

27. A fine study of an Avro 504N of the Cambridge University Air Squadron, revealing details of the aircraft's Armstrong Siddeley Lynx powerplant. The 504N was the first new trainer to be adopted by the RAF after the First World War and was built in considerable numbers, remaining in production as late as 1932. Note the two underwing gravity fuel tanks.

28. E9268 was built by the Grahame-White Aviation Co. as an Avro 504K but was later converted to 504N configuration. Avros were ideal training machines and performed sterling service with RAF units until the advent of the equally popular Tiger Moth. (Bruce Robertson)

▲25   ▼26

F.8713.

▲29

29. Another popular trainer was the Avro Tutor. The aircraft replaced the 504N at the Central Training School and proved to be a good aerobatic platform. Some pilots considered the type rather docile for a trainer, although its powerful Lynx radial was useful in teaching the operation of high-performance engines. (RAF Museum)

30. A number of Armstrong Whitworth Siskin Mk. IIIas were produced as dual-control, two-seat trainers, but they saw limited use. As can be seen, the twin-cockpit version was rather unpleasing to the eye but, nonetheless, many pilots converted successfully to the Siskin fighter as a result of experience in the trainer version. (RAF Museum)

▼30

31. A total of 47 Siskin IIIa two-seaters were eventually built; this in-flight study emphasizes the increased tail area and raised cockpit for the instructor. Roundels are applied to the lower surfaces of the upper wings rather than to the lower wing panels, as standard for the aircraft's sesquiplane wing configuration. (RAF Museum)

32. Hawker's Tomtit was one of the trend-setters in the changeover from wood to metal construction and featured the steel tube fuselage structure that was to become a Hawker hallmark up to the advent of the Hurricane. The Tomtit was an ideal trainer but saw comparatively little service and was on the strength of only two schools. (RAF Museum)

33. The first non-stop flight from England to South Africa was made by this Fairey Long-Range Monoplane, flown by Sqn. Ldr. O. R. Gayford and Flt. Lt. G. E. Nicholetts, 6–8 February 1933. The flight of nearly 5,500 miles, from Cranwell to Walvis Bay, South-West Africa, took 57hrs 25mins, establishing a world long distance record. (Ian D. Huntley)

▲34 ▼35

36 ▲

34. A rarely published close-up view of the record-breaking Fairey Long-Range Monoplane K1991. The neatly cowled Napier Lion XIA engine is noteworthy, as are the enormous wheel spats, sturdy undercarriage and wide wing chord. (Ian D. Huntley)

35. Capt. Norman Macmillan stands before Fairey Long-Range Monoplane J9479 at Northolt after its first flight on 30 October 1928. In this aircraft, Sqn. Ldr. A. G. Jones and Flt. Lt. N. H. Jenkins undertook the first non-stop flight from England to India, 24–26 April 1929, covering over 4,100 miles and reaching Karachi in 50hrs 37mins. (Ian D. Huntley)

36. In June 1937, Flt. Lt. M. J. Adam, of the Royal Aircraft Establishment at Farnborough, regained the world altitude record for heavier-than-air craft in the Bristol 138 monoplane. The 138 was powered by a special Bristol Pegasus engine fitted with a two-stage supercharger which pushed the aircraft to almost 53,940ft. A pressurized (and cumbersome) suit had to be worn by the pilot.

37. Designed primarily for research purposes, the Westland Hill Pterodactyl IV was an unconventional, high-wing, three-seat cabin monoplane powered by an inverted De Havilland Gipsy III engine mounted as a pusher. The genesis of the design could be traced back to the early 1920s when Capt. G. T. R. Hill began a study of aircraft design with the sole object of achieving stability and control at low speeds. These ideals were realized in the Pterodactyls, but the aircraft never entered series production. (Bruce Robertson)

37 ▼

38, 39. Delivery of airframes during the 1930s was a much less difficult operation than it is nowadays. Here, at the Fairey Aviation Co. factory at Hayes in Middlesex, a Thornycroft truck prepares to tow a Fairey IIIF Mk. IV. This particular aircraft, J9825 (F1223), was later converted for use as a trainer. (Ian D. Huntley)

40. This unlikely looking machine is an Avro 55A Bison Mk. II, one of eighteen ordered in July 1924. Proving the old flier's adage that 'if it looks right, it *is* right', the Bison didn't, and wasn't. Note the ladder for access to the cockpit, hardly a feature to improve aerodynamics! (RAF Museum)

▲41 ▼42

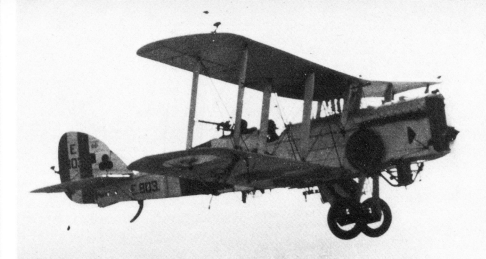

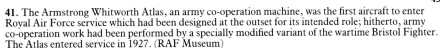

43▲

41. The Armstrong Whitworth Atlas, an army co-operation machine, was the first aircraft to enter Royal Air Force service which had been designed at the outset for its intended role; hitherto, army co-operation work had been performed by a specially modified variant of the wartime Bristol Fighter. The Atlas entered service in 1927. (RAF Museum)

42. To the Cierva C.30 Autogiro belongs the distinction of being the first rotary-wing aircraft to enter RAF service. Six of these machines were delivered to Old Sarum, Wiltshire, in December 1934, joining the strength of the School of Army Co-operation. Powered by a 140hp Armstrong Siddeley Genet Major, the Cierva was also built under licence by Avro. (RAF Museum)

43. A real, reliable workhorse, both at home and abroad in the years following the Armistice, the DH9A ('Nine-Ack') was the RAF's standard day bomber until the late 1920s. This Middle East-based aircraft carries, typically, spare wheels lashed to the undercarriage and fuselage. Note that the unit marking – the clover leaf of No. 208 Squadron – is repeated under the lower wing. (RAF Museum)

44. The Blackburn Shark was the last of a line of Blackburn torpedo biplanes operated by the Fleet air Arm but it enjoyed less than four years of front-line operational service before it was replaced by the Fairey Swordfish in 1938. The Shark was built with both wheeled undercarriage and floats. (RAF Museum)

44▼

▲45

▲46 ▼47

45. 'Worse things happen at sea . . .' A rather badly bent Blackburn Shark is winched from the sea after a misjudged landing on one of His Majesty's aircraft carriers. The fate of the crew members is unknown.

46. A single-seat, carrier-borne torpedo bomber, the ungainly Blackburn Dart entered service during 1923 and did not boast a high performance; nevertheless, it did contribute much towards the techniques of torpedo dropping. The last Darts were retired from Fleet Air Arm service in 1933. (RAF Museum)

47. The long-serving and much-loved Bristol F2B Fighter. Known as the 'Brisfit', the aircraft was the backbone of the RAF army co-operation units in the years following the Armistice and later served as a dual-control trainer and with the University Air Squadrons. (RAF Museum)

48. A splendid study of a 'Brisfit' in the Middle East during the late 1920s; the headgear of the crew should dispel any doubts as to the theatre of operations! This particular aircraft sports a replacement lower port aileron, as evidenced by the differing proportions of the RAF cockade. (RAF Museum)

49. K1118 was a Fairey IIIF Mk. IV M/A and is seen here at an air pageant in the 1920s. Ordered for the general-purpose and bombing roles and fitted with wheels for the RAF and with interchangeable wheel/float undercarriages for the FAA, the Fairey IIIF was produced in considerable numbers. Oddly, the first RAF deliveries were made to No. 47 Squadron at Khartoum, to which unit floats were subsequently supplied for operations from the River Nile. (Ian D. Huntley)

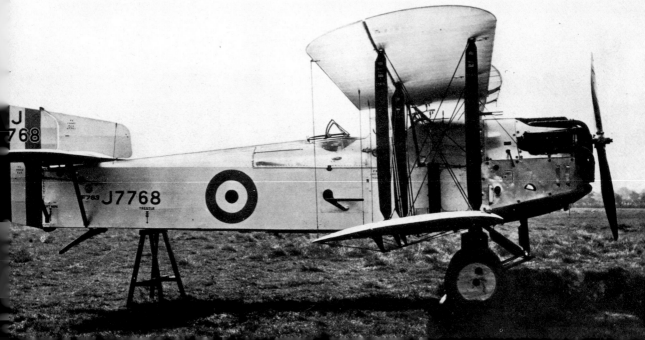

50. The Fairey IIIF design was uprated during the early 1930s to meet demands for improved performance. Re-engined with Armstrong Siddeley Panther radials, the RAF's IIIFs were designated Gordons from a standard designed as the IIIF Mk. V, whilst the Fleet received the IIIF Mk. VI (built with Panthers installed) to become the Fairey Seal. One of the latter is illustrated. (Ian D. Huntley)

51. The first of the new light day bombers in the years of cut-backs following the 1914–18 war, the Fairey Fawn entered service with the RAF in 1924 and eventually equipped five squadrons. Note the highly polished metal areas and what appears to be a variable-pitch airscrew on this example. (Ian D. Huntley)

52. Another type often overlooked is this sleek two-seat fleet fighter developed during 1928. The Fairey Fleetwing was powered by a 525hp Rolls-Royce Kestrel engine and was built to Air Ministry Specification 22/26. The aircraft could also be fitted with floats. (Ian D. Huntley)

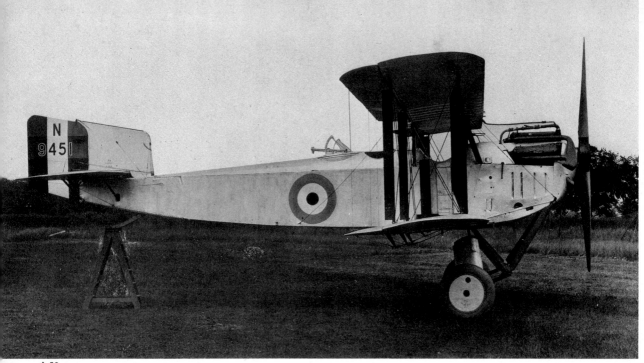

▲53

53. Factory-fresh Fairey IIID N9451, not yet fitted with its armament. The unusual arrangement of the exhaust pipes is noteworthy, as is the style of the tailfin and undercarriage, the basic design of which was incorporated on many Fairey aircraft of the period. (Ian D. Huntley)

54. The Fairey factory at Hayes turns out Seals at a cracking pace. This view of the assembly shop is full of interest for those with a keen eye for detail. The complex structure of these aircraft makes a nonsense of the 'stick and string' description so often applied to vintage aircraft types. (Ian D. Huntley)

▼54

55. In 1925 Fairey produced the revolutionary Fox two-seat day bomber. Faster than most contemporary fighters, the aircraft was aptly named. No. 12 Squadron was to operate the type and adopted a fox mask as its badge, along with the motto 'Leads the Field'. To this day the squadron's aircraft bear the fox motif. (Ian D. Huntley)

56. The Fairey IIIF Mk. IV featured a tailplane of more pleasing appearance than that of other types from its stable. This particular machine, J9154, was powered by the Jaguar VI engine. The fuselage upper decking on most silver-finished aircraft was doped either black or dark green to reduce the sun glare that might distract pilot and observer. (Ian D. Huntley)

57. The Seal Mk. I, Fairey's popular spotter/reconnaissance machine, was a large aeroplane for a single-engined type. Points of interest include the linked ailerons, the lifting rods at the rear fuselage trestle points, the capacious rear cockpit and the legends on each strut identifying its position. (Ian D. Huntley)

58. A gunner/observer aboard a Fairey Seal draws a bead on an imaginary foe. The Lewis machine gun remained virtually standard equipment long after the war had ended, although methods of mounting improved considerably. Note the sprung foot flaps in the fuselage and the clean exit guides for the elevator cables. (Ian D. Huntley)

59. The Great Western Aerodrome, c1935, is the backdrop for this study of the prototype Fairey Swordfish. During the Second World War, the Swordfish would perform feats of arms well beyond its designers' wildest dreams. Even its 'modernized' replacement, the Albacore, proved inferior. (Ian D. Huntley)

57▶

▼58

▲ 60

▲ 61 ▼ 62

60. A formation of Hawker Harts sporting the red and yellow markings of No. 601 (County of London) Squadron, Royal Auxiliary Air Force, in 1935, some time after the unit assumed its fighter role. The Hart is considered by many historians to have been one of the finest military aircraft of its day. (RAF Museum)

61. A Hawker Hart with a full warload shows off its classic lines. First flown in 1928, the Hart boasted a performance far superior to that of any fighter aircraft then extant, or on order, with the possible exception of its stablemate, the Hawker Fury. The first of 22 units to receive the type was No. 33 Squadron. (RAF Museum)

62. K2119 was an 'Indian' Hawker Hart, seen here patrolling the air space of that country and thought to be from either No. 11 or No. 39 Squadron of No. 2 (Indian) Wing. Note the appropriate headgear ('Baghdad bowlers') of the crew. Harts from these units made annual flights over the Himalayas from Risalpur to Gilgit, Kashmir, on 'show the flag' exercises. (RAF Museum)

63. A Hawker Hart, believed to be from No. 12 Squadron. From the basic Hart design were developed the Audax, Demon, Hardy, Osprey and Hector, all of which were supplied to the RAF in considerable numbers for a wide range of duties. A further variant, the Hartbees, was built for the South African Air Force. (Bruce Robertson)

64. This Hawker Hector was one of 100 examples built by Westland Aircraft. The Hector is easily distinguishable from its brethren by the redesigned cowling necessary to enclose the 805hp Napier Dagger 24-cylinder engine. Hectors were produced in considerable numbers for the air rearmament programme of the late 1930s. (RAF Museum)

65. K4462 was one of several standard Hawker Harts sold to the South African Air Force. Note the large, clear fuselage panel fitted to improve interior illumination for the pilot. This particular aircraft was one of 59 Harts in the K4437–4495 serial batch constructed by Armstrong Whitworth. (RAF Museum)

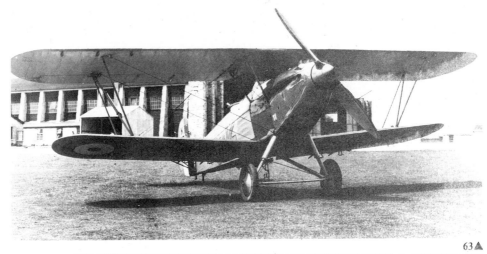

63 ▲

64 ▲ 65 ▼

66. The 'navalized' version of the Hart was the Hawker Osprey, one example of which is seen here being hoisted on to a ship's catapult. Among several distinguishing features are the long exhaust pipe and extra struts from the fuselage to support the lower wing. A number of Ospreys were actually constructed of stainless steel. (RAF Museum)

67. An interesting view of a Hawker Osprey undergoing maintenance; the location, date and unit are not known. The highly polished metal panels around the nose were painted in a form of anodized pale grey paint to resist salt water corrosion. Note the extra fuselage struts and the style of gun mounting. (RAF Museum)

68. The Hawker Woodcock. Aircraft from the second production batch were the first to enter RAF service, delivery to No. 3 Squadron at Upavon in Wiltshire being made during May 1925. The only other unit to operate the type was No. 17 Squadron, one of whose Woodcocks was borrowed by Charles Lindbergh to fly back to France from Britain shortly after his historic Atlantic crossing in 1927. (RAF Museum)

69. A Hawker Horsley comes into land. The Horsley was originally designed to meet the requirements of a 1923 specification for a medium day bomber, but its large size and good load-carrying capabilities were such that it was able to cope not only with a revised specification of 1925 but also with a contemporary requirement for a torpedo-bomber. Horsleys were used by seven RAF units and served until 1934. (RAF Museum)

70. J9640 was a Fairey IIIF Mk. IV, one of a production batch of 45 machines ordered in July 1928. In the early 1930s a spate of accidents involving IIIFs was investigated and it was found, on spinning tests, that the aircraft showed no signs of recovering from such a manoeuvre, the test crew escaping by parachute. This alarming trait was never completely cured and if a IIIF floatplane spun below a height of 1,500ft it was service doctrine for the crew to jump! (Ian D. Huntley)

▲66   ▼67

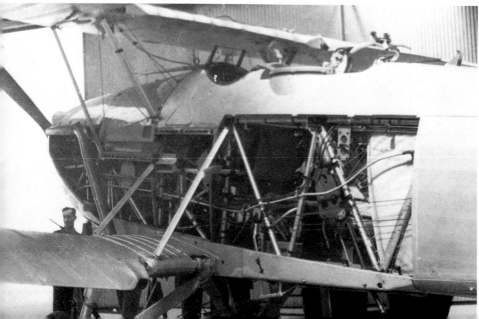

68▲

69▲   70▼

▲71

71. HRH the Prince of Wales aboard SR1174, a rebuilt Fairey IIIF Mk. I, at Khartoum during a royal tour which began on 13 April 1930. This particular aircraft belonged to No. 47 Squadron and was rebuilt from a Fleet Air Arm machine by RAF Maintenance Depot 1, based in Egypt, on 3 March 1930; these details are stencilled in black on the fin. (Ian D. Huntley)

72. A Fairey IIID of the Fleet Air Arm – note the hoisting straps on the upperwing centre-section. This rare air-to-air view emphasizes several aspects of the aircraft not usually appreciated: the 'ballooning' of the wing fabric, most noticeable on the upper wings; the tiny cockpit for the observer; and the uncowled engine. The Fairey IIID had a top speed of about 120mph and an endurance of about 4½hrs. (RAF Museum)

73. The second Fairey Seafox prototype, K4305, featured a Napier Rapier VI engine (it was the only service aircraft to be so powered), and first flew from Hamble Aerodrome on 5 November 1936. The Seafox was designed as a reconnaissance seaplane and only two appeared with the wheeled undercarriage depicted. (Ian D. Huntley)

74. Another type which has been largely forgotten is the Short S10 Gurnard; this particular aircraft, N229, was powered by a Rolls-Royce FXII engine. Either wheel or float undercarriages could be fitted. (RAF Museum)

▼72

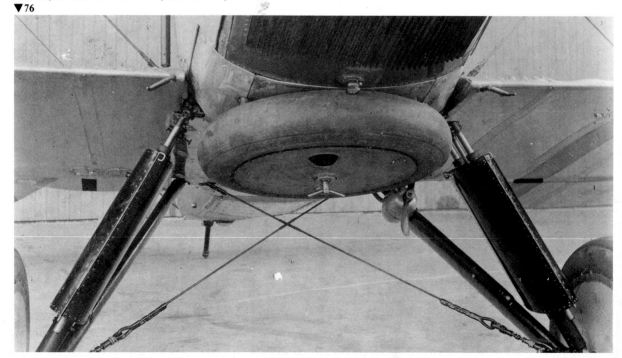

▲75

75. The Westland Wapiti was designed to embody as many DH9A components as possible in order to cut costs, but progressive modifications led to a departure from the original specification. The first production Wapitis were delivered to No. 84 Squadron at Shaibah, Iraq, during 1928. The most widely used version was the Mk. IIa, of which 430 were built. (RAF Museum)

▼76

76. A great many two-seat aircraft of the period, especially those operating over desert terrain, invariably carried spare parts whilst on patrol. This Fairey-built machine reveals one method of stowing a spare wheel under the fuselage; more than one was frequently carried. (Ian D. Huntley)

77▲

77. The Wapiti gave lengthy and valuable RAF service both at home and overseas, and came into its own during the difficult years in India and Iraq between the world wars. A number of aircraft saw service in the early months of the Second World War, as did the Wallace, a refined development. (Bruce Robertson)

78. The Blackburn Shark in its element, taxying alongside the Royal Navy warship from which this interesting photograph was taken. In common with many other service aircraft of the time, 'walk' areas on lower wings were indicated by a series of small foot-prints painted either black or dark grey.

78▼

79. The Fairey IIID floatplane was amongst the best-known and most widely used types of its day; first appearing in August 1920, it was simply constructed, tough and extremely reliable. The type saw extensive service and was used for many long-distance proving flights in the Middle East and in Africa. (Ian D. Huntley)

80. This impressive flying boat is the Fairey Atlanta, powered by four Condor 700hp engines. This particular aircraft, N119, was built by Dick Kerr Ltd. in 1920, but production orders were not forthcoming and the Atlanta never saw operational use with the Royal Air Force. (Ian D. Huntley)

81. A Fairey IIIF Mk. 2, unit unknown. During the 1931 Cyprus riots Fairey IIIFs from No. 14 Squadron, deployed in support of the Trans-Jordan Frontier Force, fired their guns on several occasions to disperse recalcitrant tribesmen. All IIIFs had been declared obsolete for RAF and FAA service by the beginning of 1940. (Ian D. Huntley)

82. Another 'rare bird'. Fairey Fremantle N173 (F429) was designed as a long-range reconnaissance floatplane and was powered by a 650hp Rolls-Royce Condor. It was designed in 1922 for a projected trans-world flight, but construction was not completed until 1925 and the aircraft was subsequently given the civil registration G-EBLZ; as such it was registered to the Air Council, flown in service markings as shown and later handed over to the RAE for radio navigation work. (Ian D. Huntley)

▲83

83, 84. The Fairey Seafox served with Nos. 702, 713, 714, 716 and 718 Catapult Flights and Nos. 753 and 754 Training Squadrons, although the former units were pooled in January 1940 to form No. 700 Squadron. A Seafox played an important part in the first major naval clash of the Second World War, when, on 13 December 1939, the cruisers *Ajax*, *Achilles*, and *Exeter* engaged the German pocket battleship *Graf Spee*. *Ajax*'s Seafox spotted for the cruisers' guns throughout the Battle of the River Plate and on 17 December reported that the *Graf Spee* had scuttled herself outside Montevideo. The Seafox pilot, Lt. E. D. G. Lewin, was awarded the DSC for his part in the action. The last British aircraft to be designed as a seaplane, the Seafox remained in service until 1943. (Ian D. Huntley)

▼84

85, 86. Although the Fairey Swordfish is generally remembered as a carrier-borne strike aircraft, many were fitted with floats. The true prototype, the TSR II, first flew on 17 April 1934 and the Swordfish entered service in the early part of summer 1936, remaining in production until 1944 and in front-line service for a further year; although obsolescent when war came in 1939, it served with distinction in a wide number of roles throughout the conflict. Easy to fly and viceless, the Swordfish was popular with its crews, who also appreciated its inherent strength. (Ian D. Huntley)

87. A flight of Short Singapores against a rather inappropriate background. One of the most elegant flying boats ever used by the RAF, the Singapore was initially issued singly to boat squadrons for training use, the first of seven operational units to become fully equipped with the type being No. 203 Squadron during August 1935. During the Spanish Civil War, boats from Nos. 209 and 210 Squadrons flew several anti-piracy patrols. (RAF Museum)

88. On 29 September 1931, Supermarine S6B S1596, with its Rolls-Royce 'R' engine boosted to 2,600hp, was flown by Flt. Lt. Stainforth at 407.5mph, thus gaining the world's speed record for Great Britain. Today this historic machine, one of the forerunners of the Spitfire, survives as one of the valuable aircraft currently on exhibition at London's Science Museum. (RAF Museum)

89. Supermarine S6 N248 was built for the 1929 Schneider Trophy contest and was later converted to S6A specification. Flying the aeroplane during the race was Flt. Lt. D'Arcy A. Grieg, who achieved almost 370mph down the 'straight' at one stage but was subsequently disqualified for making a turn inside one of the marking pylons. Two years later Flt. Lt. John Boothman, in a 2,350hp Supermarine S6B, captured the trophy for Great Britain for all time, clocking up 440.08mph. (RAF Museum)

◀87

88▲ 89▼

▲90 ▼91

90. S1152 was a Supermarine Southampton of No. 205 Squadron. The Southampton was the first flying boat of post-First World War design to enter RAF service, and five squadrons were equipped with the type. Four Southampton IIs of the Far East Flight, led by Gp. Capt. H. M. Cave-Brown-Cave, made a remarkable 27,000-mile flight between 14 October and 11 December 1928. (RAF Museum)

91. Originally known as the Seagull, the Supermarine Walrus was designed and built in 1933 as a private venture amphibian capable of being catapulted from warships. The first production orders were placed by the Australian Government, and the aircraft was ordered for the RAF's Fleet Air Arm in May 1935. During the Second World War, the Walrus did sterling service on air-sea rescue duties. (RAF Museum)

92. What's the dope? Yes, they *sprayed* the roundels on even in those days! In the paintshop, white cellulose is being applied to the underside of a lower mainplane. Rings of canvas mask out the red/blue areas, and note the use of weights and distance bars, the latter to ensure concentricity of the cockade colours. (RAF Museum)

93. A tropical survival kit for Middle East service is displayed at the Fairey factory in the late 1920s. Amongst the vital items is a spare wheel, rations, water, first aid kit and tools. The picket stakes on the right were 'screwed' rather than hammered into the ground, and cord was tied securely to picket rings under the lower wings to prevent the aircraft being turned over in heavy winds. (Ian D. Huntley)

94. Radio equipment being tested prior to take off; note the trolley-load of batteries at left. Although the full serial number cannot be seen, the aircraft is believed to be an Armstrong Whitworth Atlas army co-operation machine. (RAF Museum)

92 ▲

93 ▲   94 ▼

97▲

95. A Boulton Paul P29 Sidestrand III medium bomber of No. 101 Squadron, the only unit to receive the type. The Sidestrand, despite its large dimensions and rather ungainly appearance, was remarkably manoeuvrable for a twin-engined aircraft and could be looped, spun and rolled with little difficulty. At more than one Hendon air pageant, Sidestrands thrilled crowds with their aerobatics in mock air battles with fighters. (RAF Museum)

96. A fine study of a Boulton Paul Sidestrand III in its natural element. From this type was developed the Overstrand, which became the first RAF bomber to incorporate a fully-enclosed, power-operated gun turret. The Sidestrand remained with No. 101 Squadron for several years, that unit being the RAF's sole medium bomber squadron during the period. (RAF Museum)

97. A DH10 of No. 216 Squadron based in Egypt, c1922. Ordered originally in late 1917 as a long-distance fighter for bombing/escort work, the DH10 was subsequently ordered as a bomber (in its Mk. III version) in early 1918. The type entered postwar service with No. 97 Squadron in India and No. 216 in Egypt, the former unit being renumbered No. 60 on 1 April 1920. The DH10 was declared obsolete three years later. (RAF Museum)

98. This purposeful-looking bomber is the Handley Page Hinaidi, a contemporary of the Vickers Virginia. The first Hinaidis, re-engined Hyderabads, were designated Mk. I, and the production all-metal framed Hinaidis became Mk. II. Named after military stations in India and Iraq respectively, Hyderabads and Hinaidis were largely restricted to home use during the years 1924–37. (Bruce Robertson)

98▼

▲99

99. A Handley Page HP24 Hyderabad comes to grief, date, unit, location and circumstances not known. As befitted their intended night-bombing role, most of the RAF's 'tween-wars 'heavies' forsook the standard aluminium doping in favour of NIVO, a special dark green matt finish, with white deleted from all national insignia. (RAF Museum)

100. Vickers Victorias of No. 70 Squadron made history in the winter of 1928–29 by undertaking the world's first major airlift. For two months during the Afghan rebellion Victorias flew over 28,000 miles in some of the worst weather ever recorded, carried 24,192lb of luggage and rescued over 580 people from Kabul under fire from rebel guns. Victorias normally had a crew of two and could each carry 22 troops in their capacious fuselages.

101. A Vickers Virginia Mk. X. The Virginia, in various versions, was to be the mainstay of the RAF's night-bombing squadrons for almost ten years, and it continued in front-line operations well beyond the introduction of its successor, the Handley Page Heyford. The final Virginia versions, the Mks. IX and X, were the first bombers in widespread service to carry a gunner's cockpit in the tail. (RAF Museum)

102. An interesting close-up of a Virginia bomber with proud squadron personnel displaying some of the aircraft's warload. Note the hinged forward glazing, the neat engine installation and the shadow-shaded Flight letter. The Scarff ring above the nose for Lewis gun armament differed little from First World War models. (RAF Museum)

▼100

▲103

103. J6993 became the Vickers Virginia Mk. VII prototype, hence the aluminium doped finish. The 'Vimy tailplane' is worthy of note, as is the illumination panel in the rear fuselage. Virginias formed the equipment of Nos. 7, 9, 10, 51, 58, 97, 412, 215, 500 and 502 Squadrons and were regular performers at all the Hendon Air Displays from 1925 to 1937. (RAF Museum)

104. The Virginia Mk. X, the standard service variant, boasted an all-metal airframe, ealier marks having been wholly or partly constructed of wood. The earlier machines were, by a series of progressive manufacturing modifications, flown under several mark numbers, and only 126 Virginia airframes were actually delivered to RAF units between the years 1924 and 1932. (RAF Museum)

▼104

105. ▲

105. Another aircraft which has more or less remained in obscurity was the Vickers Vannock II, a single prototype of which was produced to Air Ministry Specification B.19/27. Note the small tailplane and the large wheel spats. (RAF Museum)

106. One of the best-known RAF twin-engined bombers of the 1920s period was the Vickers FB27 Vimy, which, although developed during the 1914–18 war, arrived too late to see operational wartime service. Aside from its use by the RAF, the Vimy proved to be one of the greatest route-pioneering aircraft ever built: in 1919 Alcock and Brown, in a modified Vimy, made the first direct Atlantic air crossing, whilst a Vimy was also the first aircraft to fly from England to Australia. (RAF Museum)

106. ▼

107. Built to the same 1927 specification as the Heyford, the Fairey Hendon was ahead of its time in many respects, but despite the type's obvious superiority over contemporary biplane heavy bombers Air Ministry procrastination resulted in a delay of seven years before a contract was awarded. K1695 is seen here in its second Kestrel VI-engined form; note the Fairey Fox in the background. (Ian D. Huntley)

▲108

108. Although it was the last biplane bomber to be used by the Royal Air Force, the Handley Page Heyford nevertheless incorporated a number of advanced features. Particular importance was attached to the rapid re-arming and refuelling of the aircraft between sorties, and a retracting 'dustbin' turret was installed under the rear fuselage. Amongst the important experiments in which Heyfords participated were the first-ever tests of airborne radar, which took place during December 1936. (RAF Museum)

109. An extremely rare view of the pilot's controls and instruments of a Fairey Hendon – simple and spartan, even for the standards of the day. A placard to the right of the compass warns the pilot not to exceed the maximum speed of 97mph, and at the extreme right is the bomb jettison switch. (Ian D. Huntley)

▼109

110. The unusual cross-section of the Hendon's fuselage is seen to advantage in this view of K1695, the prototype. Originally powered by Bristol Jupiters, the prototype was subsequently re-engined twice with Kestrel IIISs and VIs. (Ian D. Huntley)

111. The Rolls-Royce Kestrel installation in the Fairey Hendon was neat, to say the least. Plenty of detail can be seen in this unusual study, which reveals such interesting features as the wing fuel tanks, the stitched fabric panels, the large wheel fairings and the stencilling over the NIVO green finish. The 'W/T' marking, applied to all main components and moving surfaces, indicated the earthing of airframe assemblies to prevent static interference with wireless transmission or risk of fire. (Ian D. Huntley)

▲ 112

112. Mid-March 1936 is the date for this photograph of K4303, the prototype Fairey Battle. Towards the end of the 1930s, fast new monoplane types were slowly replacing the venerable biplane designs, and as war clouds gathered in Europe the RAF could look forward to more sophisticated, more modern machines for their squadrons. Even so, the Battle was sorely outclassed when the Second World War broke out, and it was soon withdrawn from front-line use. (Ian D. Huntley)

113. Where a legend began. K2890 was the Supermarine Type 224 'Day and Night Fighter', designed and built to Air Ministry Specification F.7/30. The 224 more or less bridged the gap between the S6B and the Spitfire, and its main function was to reveal to the designer what features were necessary for a high-speed fighter. Many valuable lessons were learnt, and two years after the 224 first flew, in February 1934, the prototype Spitfire took to the skies. (RAF Museum)

▼113